GALAXY OF SUPERSTARS

Ben Affleck

Backstreet Boys

Garth Brooks

Mariah Carey

Cameron Diaz

Leonardo DiCaprio

Tom Hanks

Hanson

Jennifer Love Hewitt

Lauryn Hill

Ewan McGregor

Mike Myers

'N Sync

LeAnn Rimes

Britney Spears

Spice Girls

Jonathan Taylor Thomas

Venus Williams

CHELSEA HOUSE PUBLISHERS

GALAXY OF SUPERSTARS

Garth Brooks

Stacey L. Stauffer

CHELSEA HOUSE PUBLISHERS
Philadelphia

Frontis: *Sometimes quiet and intense, often joyous and exuberant, Garth Brooks has sung and played his way to the top of his career as a country music entertainer.*

Produced by
21st Century Publishing and Communications, Inc.
New York, New York
http://www.21cpc.com

CHELSEA HOUSE PUBLISHERS

Editor in Chief: Stephen Reginald
Managing Editor: James D. Gallagher
Production Manager: Pamela Loos
Art Director: Sara Davis
Director of Photography: Judy L. Hasday
Senior Production Editor: LeeAnne Gelletly
Publishing Coordinator: James McAvoy
Assistant Editor: Anne Hill
Cover Designer: Keith Trego

Front Cover Photo: Ron Wolfson/London Features Int'l
Back Cover Photo: Ron Wolfson/London Features Int'l

The Chelsea House World Wide Web address is
http://www.chelseahouse.com

First Printing

1 3 5 7 9 8 6 4 2

Library of Congress Cataloging-in-Publication Data

Stauffer, Stacey, 1973–
   Garth Brooks / by Stacey L. Stauffer.
   64 p. cm. – (Galaxy of superstars)
   Includes bibliographical references and index.
   Summary: A biography of the country music entertainer who has sold millions
of albums and won countless awards including the Academy of Country Music's
"Artist of the Decade."
   ISBN 0-7910-5232-X — ISBN 0-7910-5332-6 (pbk)
   1. Brooks, Garth—Juvenile literature. 2. Country musicians—United States—
Biography—Juvenile literature. [1. Brooks, Garth. 2. Country musicians.]
I. Title. II. Series.
ML3930.B855S73 1999
782.42164'092—dc21
[B]   99—32951
                                                                                      CIP
                                                                                       AC

Dedication: To my Chincoteague family, who has shown me that country is unconditional love, faith, and nonstop fun. Are you ready for the "new place?" And to the O.H.S. gang—thanks for the music and for making those years some of the best. You have proven to me that friends and family are forever and that God has made it all possible. I love you all. Dad, thanks for giving us the best childhood. I couldn't imagine life without the farm. Shawn, Scott, Pam—there's not much we wouldn't do for GB, is there?!?! *We've gone country.*

Contents

Chapter 1
The Entertainer   7

Chapter 2
The Boy from Oklahoma   13

Chapter 3
Stillwater   19

Chapter 4
A Second Shot   25

Chapter 5
More Than Just a Dance   33

Chapter 6
"Country Conquers Rock"   41

Chapter 7
This Is Garth Brooks   49

Chronology   59
Discography   60
Awards   60
Further Reading   63
Index   64

THE ENTERTAINER

For the fourth time that evening Garth Brooks walked up on the stage to accept an award—the one he had been waiting for. Hosted by Reba McEntire, the Country Music Association (CMA) was holding its 25th annual awards ceremony in October 1991. More than 33 million viewers saw the ceremony, which came in first in the television ratings for the week and was the second highest-rated special of the 1991–92 season. The event is, as country music star Martina McBride described to *People Weekly*, ". . . our biggest night of the year. Our night to shine."

Just the year before, Garth's country music rival, Clint Black, had overshadowed Brooks in most of the award categories. Now it was Garth's turn to shine. He received awards for Best Video of the Year for his controversial *Thunder Rolls*. His album *No Fences* was selected as the Best Album of the Year, and his high-spirited song "Friends in Low Places" had picked up the Best Single award. The last award presented is always

---

For his legions of fans, Garth Brooks is the King of Country Music, and his countless awards acknowledge him as country music's top entertainer. His honors include the prestigious Entertainer of the Year award, bestowed by the Academy of Country Music, and four highly coveted Entertainer of the Year awards from the Country Music Association.

the most prestigious. For the Country Music Association the final award is Entertainer of the Year.

Overcome with emotion as Garth accepted his first CMA Entertainer of the Year award, he was also excited and joyous. Garth displayed the humble attitude for which he has become famous. "This is cool," he said. "It's funny how a chubby kid can just be having fun and they call it entertaining." The singer had established himself as a talented newcomer when he won the Horizon Award and Best Video of the Year in 1990, and now he had defined himself as a major player in the country music genre. Over the next eight years, Garth would have three more opportunities to accept this celebrated award. He recently admitted that it was a prize he truly had striven to achieve. "Goals always change. When you first start out, it's to hear your song on the radio. Then once that happens, it's to get a shiny gold album. Then it's the CMA Award," explained the four-time CMA Entertainer of Year.

Nineteen ninety-one was an exciting year for this novice to the music industry. Earlier in the year, Garth had picked up six awards from the Academy of Country Music (ACM), including best video, song, single record, and album, and was also honored as ACM's Male Vocalist of the Year and Entertainer of the Year. Throughout the next several years, Garth would get plenty of practice giving acceptance speeches. Still, each time was an emotional experience for him. In 1992, when Garth once again received the CMA's Entertainer of the Year award, he was overcome with tears as

he was embraced by country music legend Johnny Cash.

Garth's sincerity has always been obvious when accepting an award. Often he must regain his composure before he can speak. At other times he recognizes those who have been his role models in the industry. During the 1991 CMA awards, in front of an audience that included President George Bush and First Lady Barbara Bush, Brooks acknowledged two Georges—Strait and Jones—as his

Garth's unique and often rousing performance style captures and excites audiences everywhere. Getting close to his fans is part of a Garth Brooks concert, and they respond enthusiastically.

Even as a superstar, Garth has never lost his delight in his fans' appreciation for his music. After being introduced to a screaming audience by Jay Leno on The Tonight Show, *Garth salutes his fans with a heartfelt bow.*

vocal heroes. He quickly added, "No offense, Mr. President."

Later in his career, Garth surprised the 1996 ACM audience with his endearing behavior after winning the Favorite Artist of the Year award. Making his way to the stage, Garth shook hands with and hugged Boyz II Men and Hootie and the Blowfish who, among others, had also been nominated in the same category. When presented with the award by

Neil Diamond, Garth delivered a quite unexpected speech:

> Thank you very much. So you'll know right off the bat, I cannot . . . agree with this. Music is made up of a lot of people. And if we're one artist short, then we all become a lesser music. So, without any disrespect to the American Music Awards, and without any disrespect to any fans who voted. For all the people who should be honored with this award, I'm gonna leave it right here. Thank you very much.

He then walked quietly off the stage, leaving the award on the podium as promised.

Since his career first took off in 1989, Garth Brooks has become the king of country music. And through his unique and genuine passion for the music, he has also captured the ears and eyes, and hearts, of many non-country fans.

2

THE BOY
FROM OKLAHOMA

Troyal Garth Brooks entered the world on February 7, 1962, in Tulsa, Oklahoma, becoming the eighth member of the Brooks family. His mother, Colleen Carroll Brooks, had three children from a previous marriage, and his father, Troyal Raymond Brooks, had one child from his first marriage. Colleen and Raymond also had two children of their own, first Kelly and then Garth. Although four of Garth's siblings were stepbrothers and stepsisters, his parents made sure that all of their children felt connected and did not feel separate from one another. In Colleen's and Raymond's eyes, they had six children who were all brothers and sisters.

Raymond Brooks was an engineer and draftsman. Although he was also a former marine who could be intimidating, he actually was a loving, gentle man. Garth shared an important message he learned from his father: ". . . you gotta be thankful for what you got. And you gotta treat people like you want to be treated." Although Garth inherited many of his father's qualities, such as a big heart and the ability to pick up the guitar and sing,

---

Garth's home state is known for its fields of wheat. It is also famous for raising country music entertainers. The young boy from Oklahoma had no idea that one day his name would be emblazoned across 50 acres of an Oklahoma wheat field in letters 300 feet tall.

the boy's interest in country music can be mostly credited to his mother. Colleen had been a featured singer on Red Foley's weekly radio and television show, *Ozark Jubilee*, in Nashville and had also recorded singles for Capitol Records. When she met Raymond, however, she agreed to give up her music career and move to Oklahoma. Garth attributes much of his pursuit of his music dream to his mother. As he has explained, "We kids felt that she had cut her career short because of us. We wanted to carry on the tradition for her."

When Garth was four, his family moved to Yukon, a small city not far from Oklahoma City. As a young boy, Garth was popular at school and, according to his third-grade teacher, loved music and getting attention from girls. Music was a part of the Brooks's home, and everyone played the guitar, the harmonica, sang, or performed something musical to entertain one another. In fact, they had a weekly ritual called Funny Night, at which time the family would sing, perform skits, or do imitations. Since Garth was the youngest in the family, he wasn't able to do much musically. Still, Garth's sister Betsy remembers his desire to perform even then, "Garth would want right in the middle of it, and he'd capture your attention."

As Garth grew up, however, he began devoting his attention to other interests. Although he received a banjo for his 16th birthday and loved to play around with music, he was mostly interested in being a "Miller"—a jock on Yukon high school's sports teams. He played basketball, baseball, football, was on the track and field team, and dreamed of becoming a sports

star. Garth gives the credit to his father for his competitive nature, which made sports a natural for him. His father, he recalled, taught him that he didn't need to always win but that he had to give it his best shot. "I've always been raised that no matter what you do, if you're not out to be the best, don't go out there and do it," Garth has said. He has relied on this advice throughout his life despite some hard times when he would be tested to see if he had the courage to "go out there and do it."

Surrounded by family and friends, Garth's dreams were formed in his happy home on Yukon Avenue. Raymond and Colleen had cultivated an atmosphere that allowed their

Growing up surrounded by a loving family, Garth was encouraged by his parents to form his own dreams for his future. Close to his mother, Colleen, shown here answering phones at a charity function, Garth never fails to acknowledge the love and support she has given him.

children to think for themselves, to make their own decisions. He later described his family life as "totally cool. . . . You could try things—stretch your imagination. It was a house you could make mistakes in."

As a teen, Garth was attracted to a wide variety of music. He enjoyed the performances of hard rock groups, the soft lyrics of more contemporary pop music, and of course country music. He was also drawn to the wild antics performed during the concerts of harder rock groups such as Kiss and Queen. In fact, it was these groups that would inspire Garth's own erratic behavior while performing live, and which contributed to his ability to captivate audiences with his unique performance style.

Although country music attracted Garth, it was not until college that he would realize that he wanted to pursue a career as a country singer. Some of Garth's fellow high-school classmates were in fact surprised that music was to become his calling in life. One friend, Reese Wilson, remembered that Garth was less interested in music and in country music than most other students: "He started later than we did. We were all ready to play music, and he was just learning what was going on. Garth was kind of a jock. And when he did get into music, it was mainly rock. When I first heard Garth on the radio, I wasn't sure it was the same guy." Others, however, remember it differently, recalling that music was a large part of Garth's home life and that he often tried to get bands together with his high-school buddies.

Garth was a good student, and his parents,

knowing the importance of education, encouraged him and all of their children to go on to college. Five of them did. Money could be a problem, however, for a family that had to "scrape the bottom of the barrel a lot of times," as Colleen recalled. For Garth, it was his excellence in sports that earned him a track scholarship to Oklahoma State University when he graduated from high school in 1980. Taking the scholarship, he followed his brother Kelly to Oklahoma State University in Stillwater.

3

STILLWATER

Although Oklahoma State University (OSU) was not far from Yukon, getting away from his hometown gave Garth an outlet to find out more about himself and to begin pursuing other interests, mainly music. Stillwater was to become a special place for Garth because it was there that his musical dream was born. In honor of his university town, Garth has named his present band Stillwater.

At OSU, Garth and his brother Kelly were roommates and enjoyed spending time together. Garth even told his mother, "I could live with Kelly 24 hours a day." Neither young man smoked or drank or indulged in rowdy college get-togethers. Although their family did not attend church, Garth and his brother accepted a faith that is evident in the lyrics of the songs Garth writes today. His mother recalls that "When Kelly and Garth were at OSU, they had the whole athletic dorm returning thanks [at meals]."

Garth continued track and field in college, becoming good at javelin throwing, but he was not exceptional. He realized that his dreams of being a sports star would not come true. Instead he turned to his musical talents.

"Bringing Dreams to Life," as the sign at Oklahoma State University proclaims, could have been the motto for young Garth Brooks as he entered college. Although he had an athletic scholarship, he renewed his passion for music at Stillwater and began the musical career that has taken him to stardom.

During his freshman year, he played guitar with other students. Garth got a break when as a sophomore he was chosen to represent his dorm in the university's talent contest. On April 6, 1982, Garth experienced his first musical success after winning the $50 first prize. He sang three songs by Dan Fogelberg, and it was obvious to everyone that he had a beautiful voice and that the guitar was his instrument. "He could chord around on the mandolin and banjo, but the acoustic guitar was his main thing," said old friend Jim Harris. "He knew thousands of chords. . . . a lot of the songs . . . had some pretty difficult chord patterns." At this point, Garth did not plan to pursue a musical career. Since he was majoring in marketing and advertising and had been exceptionally good at English in high school, he hoped to find a job writing pitches or jingles for commercials.

To make some extra money to help cover his college expenses and to exercise his musical talents, Garth began performing at local restaurants and bars. His first musical gig was at Shotgun Sam's Pizza Parlor. He also played at Wild Willie's Saloon, making about $100 for each four-hour performance. Since it was not enough to cover all of his expenses, Garth also took a job as a bouncer at a nightclub called Tumbleweed and broke up any fights that occurred. At the club, he met a young woman, Sandy Mahl, who would later become his wife.

The circumstances of how they met were a bit unusual. Sandy had gotten into a fight with another woman. Garth the bouncer broke up the fight and escorted Sandy from the club, at which time he asked her for a date. Sandy had grown up in Owasso, Oklahoma, a small town

From his teen years, Garth had wanted to become a star athlete. Although he was good at sports, he soon realized he would never be outstanding. His love of sports has not diminished, however. Years later he joined and worked out with the San Diego Padres baseball team, which invited him to be a nonroster player.

not far from Tulsa. A high-school cheerleader as well as a rodeo rider for a time, Sandy too had a competitive nature. Before long, she and Garth began a serious relationship. While they dated, Sandy became a strong believer in Garth's musical abilities. She remembers when he would do his gigs at the saloons: "He'd just get up and he would play anything from Neil Young to Willie Nelson, Elton John . . . or Dan Fogelberg. It was whatever anyone could yell out. He'd say, 'I don't really know that one but I'll try it.'"

Garth readily acknowledges his debt to his vocal hero and role model George Strait (right). From the moment he heard Strait sing, Garth knew that he too wanted to be a country music performer.

When Garth met Sandy, he was a junior and was already well known in town for his musical gigs. His interest in pursuing his music was growing. In addition to playing at local bars, Garth was often asked to play for private events or at a friend's party or wedding reception. He had finally decided that if he did become a singer, he wanted to perform country music. Although Garth loved a wide range of music, it was country singers such as Merle Haggard and George Jones who influenced his musical direction. The singer who had the most impact on Garth, however, was George Strait.

When Strait's first single, "Unwound," hit the radio airwaves in 1981, Garth then knew that country music was the way to go for him. "Throughout all the 1980s, I was a George Strait wannabe," he recalled.

Garth was so intent on his music, however, that he began to falter in his schoolwork. He considered dropping out of college, but his parents convinced him to finish his education. Sandy was also a source of strength for Garth. She believed Garth had what it takes to make it as a singer, and she boosted his self-confidence, encouraging him to keep working toward his goal.

When Garth graduated from Oklahoma State in December 1984, he contacted college friend Jim Harris, asking Jim to help make a demo tape of the songs he had written. Garth rounded up some background singers and other musicians, and they gathered together at a recording studio outside of Stillwater to make Garth's first demo tape.

With his tapes and his guitar, Garth decided he was ready to take his music to Nashville, Tennessee, home of so many singers and major recording and music-publishing companies. He packed up his car and, with no intention of returning, headed for "Music City, USA." He had left Sandy in Stillwater and his family in Yukon. "When I left Oklahoma, when I crossed into Arkansas," Brooks recounts dramatically, "I said, 'Good-bye, Oklahoma, I don't need you. I don't need the woman that I left behind. I don't need anybody. I'm gonna make it on my own.'" He later admitted, "I was a jerk. When I left, I didn't tell her, but I wasn't planning on coming back. I didn't think I'd see her again once I moved to Nashville."

4

A SECOND SHOT

Garth's first trip to Nashville lasted a mere 24 hours. Someone he met from the music industry quickly opened the young hopeful's eyes to the difficulties of making it big in the industry and told him how little money most musicians make starting out. Garth realized that he could make more doing small gigs back home, and he was not ready to put out the energy it would take for success in Nashville. As he later admitted, he had a fantasy about Music City, USA: "I came to Nashville thinking that opportunity just hung on trees and that all I had to do was take out my guitar and strum a little bit and sing and someone would say, 'Hey, kid, let me give you a record deal and a couple million dollars, and you can go back home.'" Garth hurried away from Nashville and went back to Stillwater empty-handed.

Despite Garth's abrupt leaving, Sandy was grateful for his return and accepted him back into her life. Within a few months, the couple became engaged and were married in May 1986. Garth worked in retail jobs, but he kept fine-tuning his musical skills with gigs at local establishments

Garth's quick rise to fame in the country music world was compared to that of many other performers. Within a year of his second trip to Nashville, he had nabbed a contract with Capitol Records, impressing its executives with his dynamic style and his unique ability to instantly connect with audiences.

in Stillwater. He also performed with a band called the Skinner Brothers, playing rock, pop, and occasionally some country. When the band broke up, Garth and some of its members reformed, calling themselves Santa Fe.

Performing gigs for colleges in the area, the band's reputation spread, spurring Garth to again follow his dream of becoming a musician. In 1987, with a wife for moral support as well as a band behind him, Garth returned to Nashville. Garth, Sandy and the band rented a house together in Hendersonville, just north of Nashville.

At first, it seemed Garth and the band had run into some luck when they met with an industry executive, Bob Doyle. A record deal failed to materialize, however, and the band split up, with many of the members returning to Oklahoma.

Garth and Sandy decided to stay in Nashville, where he managed a retail store and she worked at clerical jobs. Garth had not given up his hopes for a career in music, and he continued to meet with record companies. Eager to push ahead, Garth and Sandy were impatient for the right opportunity. Like many young, new entertainers, they had put all of their energy and hopes into getting a record deal, and they had suffered an extremely tough year.

Constant rejections were terribly discouraging, and at times Garth wanted to give it all up. It was Sandy who talked him into staying. "Look," she said, "I can't spend my life going back and forth, back and forth. We're here. Let's give it at least three years. If nothing happens, we'll go back." Garth admitted later, "I thought we weren't going to make it. I thought we were going to crash, trash out, go into debt, poverty, and stuff. It had nothing to do with music. It was two people, newly married, struggling against

True to the tradition expressed in so many country music lyrics, Garth's wife, Sandy Mahl, has "stood by her man." Despite ups and downs in their early years, she has been his mainstay and greatest supporter.

debt. I thought it was over." It was a year filled with fear, frustration, and rejection.

And then something happened. The industry executive Bob Doyle, with whom Garth had met earlier, had set up his own music-publishing company called Major Bob Music. In February 1988, Doyle signed Garth to write marketing jingles and commercials for companies such as John Deere tractors. At the same time, Doyle was marketing Garth to major record companies, none of whom seemed to be interested in the young singer's talents. Doyle persisted, however, and finally got Garth an audition with Jim Foglesong, the head of Capitol Records. A nervous Garth played and sang a number of songs for Foglesong and other Capitol Records staffers. They did not seem to be impressed, however, and Garth left with only handshakes.

A few weeks later, Doyle took Garth to the Bluebird Cafe, a place where singers and songwriters could test their talents and which attracted record executives. Initially Garth only went to see his competition, but he got an unexpected chance to perform when an originally scheduled act failed to appear. The two songs Garth played captured the audience with their emotion and intensity, just as his music has done at every performance since.

When he finished singing "If Tomorrow Never Comes," Lynn Shults, a Capitol Records executive who had been at Garth's audition, offered him a record deal on the spot. Shults apologized for not taking him more seriously when she had first heard him, admitting, "Maybe we missed something." What Shults had missed was Garth's connection with the audience. On June 17, it became official. Garth signed a contract with Capitol Records and received a $10,000 advance.

Having signed a record deal within a year of arriving in Nashville may have seemed a lifetime to Garth, but by industry standards it was almost instant recognition. Garth's work had only begun, however. Now he had to compose the songs for the album he had dreamed of creating. From the songs that Shults had heard, it was obvious that Garth would not be the traditional country singer. His charisma was unique, and his music crossed the line from country to classic rock and even to pop. Shults had to find Garth a producer who would be just as flexible. After interviewing several possible candidates, Both Garth and Shults wanted Allen Reynolds. Garth liked Reynolds after interviewing him, and Shults agreed. Shults thought Reynolds was a great choice because "I just knew he was a guy who could stretch more musically than most producers in this town."

While Garth and Reynolds worked on the album, Capitol Records was busy marketing its new singer. Garth's first single, "Much Too Young," hit the airwaves in March 1989. Although the song never passed number eight on the *Billboard* charts, it helped the newcomer to get his name recognized. The following month, Garth's first album, *Garth Brooks*, was released. It included 10 songs, half of which were written by Garth. To promote his album, Garth began touring, and he also formed his own band, Stillwater, playing in small establishments to promote his songs.

Garth brought an exciting new style to country music concerts during his initial tour. Unlike so many country singers, he didn't just hold a microphone and walk back and forth across the stage. Garth was totally animated onstage, performing stunts such as climbing up rope ladders and smashing guitars. Antics like these are part of what has made Garth such a popular music entertainer. The other reason is the extraordinary way that he connects with his audience. Garth communicates his emotions through his lyrics, through his passion for singing, and especially through his eyes.

Recognizing Garth's ability to inspire audiences, Capitol Records chose the ballad "If Tomorrow Never Comes'" as his second single release. The song proved to be the perfect choice to reveal the sensitivity of this newcomer to country music. The lyrics tell people to cherish their families and friends since they never know when their lives may end. "If Tomorrow Never Comes" was especially dear to Garth because of his own life experiences. "That song means a lot to me because of friends I've lost," Garth revealed. Not only did Garth's second single hit number one on the charts, it also helped boost sales of his album, which became the best-selling country album of the 1980s, selling more than six million copies.

Garth's career dreams were all coming true, but his personal life was in trouble. At a concert in November 1989, he was overcome with emotion and unable to finish. He apologized to the audience, saying that he was going through some tough times. Touring meant separation from Sandy for months at a time, and this long-distance relationship was straining their marriage. Sandy had also heard that while on the road, Garth had been unfaithful to her. Just before the November concert, Sandy had delivered an ultimatum—come home to straighten out their lives together or she was leaving.

Sandy has recalled this painful period when Garth flew to her side and begged her forgiveness. "He was ashamed, embarrassed, and it was written all over his face. He had hurt me so bad. I had wasted two years of my life is how I felt." Sandy forgave Garth, but not right away. "I wanted Garth to feel my pain," she explained. Realizing how difficult it was for Sandy to take him back, especially since she had supported him so loyally, Garth responded: "It took a helluva human being to forgive me. I love her to death. When I've been down, Sandy has given me strength."

Nineteen eighty-nine had held challenges for Garth Brooks. But they would not be the last he would face in his professional or personal life.

Garth is probably as famous for his wild performance antics as he is for his music. Here, he grabs the attention of an audience by soaring through the air against his gigantic image displayed in the background.

5

MORE THAN
JUST A DANCE

Once back together with Sandy, Garth needed to get his home life in order. It seemed best that he be surrounded with those who mattered most to him, so it was decided that Sandy would tour with him whenever possible. Garth also hired his brother Kelly to handle tour finances and talked his sister into becoming a background vocalist with his band.

With his family life now more stable, Garth could focus on his next career move. In 1989, his first album had hit number 12 on *Billboard* magazine's Top 200 Chart and number two on *Billboard*'s Country Chart. In April 1990, the Academy of Country Music nominated him for Top New Male Vocalist, Top Song, and Top Single. His main competitor, Clint Black, was also nominated in these same categories. Although Black edged Garth out by capturing the male vocalist and single awards, Garth had reached a high point from which he could not be toppled.

With Garth's hit ballad "The Dance" and the video that followed, the young singer was rapidly becoming a major player in the world of country music. Despite his phenomenal success, he is always ready to share the stage with other entertainers (Charlie Daniels, center, and Chris LeDoux, right). Garth especially admires LeDoux, a former rodeo star turned singer, whom Garth credits with having given him the advice that launched him on his "ride of a lifetime."

On the night before the awards ceremony, Garth enjoyed a memorable encounter with someone he greatly admired and had always wanted to meet. He performed at a club in Victorville, California, with Chris LeDoux, a rodeo star turned singer. Even now as he recalls that initial meeting with LeDoux, Garth reveals the impact it had on him: "He and his guys taught us that night that no one in the house should be louder than the band, wilder than the band, or have more fun than the band. I felt something 'click,' we all did. We had no way of knowing it then, but the ride of a lifetime was about to begin."

It wasn't only enthusiasm that fueled Garth's high spirits. He simply did not have the time to lament his loss at the awards ceremony. He was touring with Holly Dunn, opening shows for Reba McEntire, attending benefit concerts such as Farm Aid, and working on his second album. Garth was also creating a video of "The Dance," one of the singles from his first album.

The song, "The Dance," captured the essence of the singer Garth Brooks who, as he explains, does not choose or write songs that he believes will sell, but rather songs that express himself and provoke listeners to think about their own lives. Released as a single, "The Dance" was acclaimed, with *Billboard* reviewing it as "easily the most eloquently written and sensitively interpreted love song of the last decade." The song seems to be saying that even though love has gone astray, there should be no regrets about what once was because of what it gave. As the lyrics express it, we could have "missed the pain," but then we would have had to "miss the dance."

Garth liked the simplicity of those thoughts on love, but on the video he wanted to convey a deeper theme. He included figures such as John F. Kennedy, Martin Luther King Jr., John Wayne, Keith Whitley, and the crew of the space shuttle *Challenger* because they had died young and in the midst of pursuing their dreams. For Garth, "The Dance" is not only about a romantic relationship. It is about giving everything you

His eyes closed and intent on his music, Garth is captured in a quiet, serious moment. Whether sad or funny, Garth's songs hold audiences with their true country spirit.

have, including your life, to obtain your dreams.

One figure in the video who is not that well-known is Lane Frost, a bull rider who was killed in a rodeo at the age of 25. Garth chose to include Frost because Garth himself could be compared to the daring and passionate young rodeo star who was pursuing his dream when he died. Choosing Frost and the other figures gave a new interpretation to the song's lyrics. At the beginning of the video, Garth's introduction also captures viewers' attention and compels them to see Garth as more than a mere entertainer. "To a lot of people, I guess 'The Dance' is a love-gone-bad song, which, you know, that it is," he says. "To me, it's always been a song about life—or maybe the loss of, those people that have given the ultimate sacrifice for a dream that they believed in. . . . And if they could come back, I think they would say to us what the lyrics of 'The Dance' say."

In his performances as well as in interviews, Garth has acknowledged that "The Dance" is his favorite song, perhaps because it expresses his own values and beliefs. At the end of the video, Garth returns to describe his feelings: "You know, I would never compare myself with the folks that are seen in the video. But if for some reason, God forbid, I should leave this world unexpectedly, I hope they play 'The Dance' for me. I mean, that's it: I could have missed the pain, but I'd have had to miss the dance. I wouldn't miss this for the world." The song became Garth's second number-one single, and the video earned him CMA's Video of the Year award in 1990.

By October 1990, Garth's first album had sold more than one million copies, making it a certified platinum album. It would not be his biggest-selling album, however. His much-anticipated second album, *No Fences*, was released in August of that year. Four of its songs would quickly find their way to number one on the *Billboard* Country Music Chart. Garth has acknowledged that one song, the widely popular "Friends in Low Places," has become his trademark song. Although the story of an old boyfriend crashing a former love's wedding is not new, the power of the lyrics and Garth's performance of the song have made it unforgettable. Although the song is pure country—a lost love, too much drinking, friends who stand by no matter what—it landed on the pop charts and continued to attract noncountry listeners. "Friends in Low Places" is a light-hearted song that forces audiences to scream along and to laugh afterwards. As Garth has said, "When it comes to songs, I would say the biggest song for us in the '90s had to be 'Friends in Low Places.'"

Three other songs on *No Fences* also helped to make it the biggest-selling country album of all time. The amusing "Two of a Kind" and "Workin' on a Full House" expressed the fun-loving nature of this rising country star. Two additional songs that received much praise were "Unanswered Prayers" and "The Thunder Rolls," both of which Garth wrote. "The Thunder Rolls" became controversial because of its theme about an unfaithful, abusive husband whose wife fights back. Garth also made a graphic video of the song, which he realized would offend some viewers. He felt, however, that it carried an extremely important message that needed to be shown.

Because of the violence the video portrayed,
the two major country music video networks
refused to play it. It also resulted in fights
between Garth and Sandy because he played
the part of the husband, and Sandy didn't
approve of the video. But the controversy only
enhanced fans' interest and made the video
and song even more popular.

Garth's first album had laid the foundation
for his rise as a top artist. His second album
made it obvious he had become a major player
in the country music arena. Looking back at
his first album, he recalls: "I was scared to
death. When we first started, I had one thing
in mind, and that was to make folks back
home proud. I really felt like I was representing
Yukon, Oklahoma, and more than anything
I wanted them to like what I did."

Without a doubt, Yukon was proud of
Garth. During a ceremony in March 1991,
Yukon proclaimed itself as "The Home of Garth
Brooks." In addition to putting this message
on the town's water tower and on a highway
sign at the city's border, Yukon also renamed a
portion of its State Highway 92 as "Garth
Brooks Boulevard."

Shortly after the release of *No Fences*,
Garth earned a number of awards, shutting
out all other competitors in each category in
which he was nominated. Garth explained his
success simply by saying: "By the time we
recorded *No Fences*, all my fears had gone
away. I was confident and calm, it was like
stepping up to the plate and knowing that you
can hit the ball." Following the release of his
third album, *Ropin' the Wind*, in 1991, Garth
won the most coveted and prestigious award

given by the CMA—Entertainer of the Year. *Ropin' the Wind* went on to become the second largest-selling country album of all time, displacing Garth's own *No Fences* as number one, and becoming the first album ever in history to hit number one on both *Billboard's* Top 200 Pop Chart and its Country Chart.

The star's home-run streak would not end there. Garth continued pumping out absolute killer albums, unbelievable live performances, and a powerful charisma that would reward him with many more fans.

Garth has a well-deserved reputation for recognizing those who have influenced his career. Accepting an ACM Entertainer of the Year Award, Garth reaches out to George Strait and proclaims, "You're the man."

6

"COUNTRY CONQUERS ROCK"

G arth's numerous awards certainly contributed to his tremendous popularity and the rising sales of his albums. But the single major cause for his huge sales and immense appeal is believed to be his live concerts. In 1992, Garth surprised everyone by recording a televised special, *This Is Garth Brooks*, for the NBC television network.

Filmed at Reunion Arena in Dallas, Texas, where Garth had performed two sold-out concerts, the show thrilled viewers with its offbeat and dangerous antics. Right at the beginning, Garth captured his audience with his dialogue. He began by staring out at viewers and greeting them: "Hi. I'm Garth Brooks. For the next hour, I'm gonna try to show you what a Garth Brooks is. For a little head start, I'm fortunate enough to play country music for a living. I'm from the state of Oklahoma, and—*wait!*" Garth then mockingly begs his viewers to stay and watch and continued to kid them: "Where're you going? Oh, the country music thing, huh? I know what you're thinking . . . dull . . . boring . . . old hat." The show proved to be anything but.

Garth often overwhelms audiences with extravagant concerts such as this one at which his image is projected on a giant screen behind him as he performs. As a larger-than-life entertainer, he has carried country music into the mainstream and may have made it even as popular as rock.

41

While Garth speaks, clips from his concerts show viewers just how exciting this special will be. From that moment on, audiences were caught up in the performance as Garth hurled water in the air, ran and danced across the stage, and trashed two guitars by slamming them together. He was showing America that country was certainly not boring. In between concert shots, Garth, his family, and his band and crew talked about the concerts and the man behind them.

More than 28 million people tuned in that evening to learn more about this master of entertainment and the country music sensation that is Garth Brooks. The show cost about $2 million to produce, but it was the highest-rated Friday one-hour special for NBC in nine years. Millions saw Garth Brooks as a risky, friendly, and most of all, a fun-loving country boy with the charisma to attract even the most skeptical of viewers.

Garth's career was soaring, but he was considering retiring. Why? Sandy was expecting their first child, and Garth was not sure he could be a good dad with his hectic schedule. Also, Sandy had been told to rest during her pregnancy, so Garth took time off to be with her. When daughter Taylor Mayne Pearl Brooks was born on July 8, 1992, Garth continued to stay with his family, but he was not ready to retire just yet.

Although Garth laid low for awhile, his image did not. It was impossible to walk past a magazine rack and not see Garth Brooks's charming smile grace the covers of several periodicals. His picture or an article or quote about him could be found in publications

from *Entertainment Weekly* to the *New Yorker,* *Forbes, The New York Times, Playboy, Rolling Stone,* and *USA Today.* Such overwhelming attention proved that Garth Brooks had surely become mainstream. The *Forbes* article even declared "Country Conquers Rock." Although the majority of the reports were positive, some did criticize Garth and his music. Whether it was positive or negative, however, it was still publicity and did nothing to hurt the ever-popular star's career.

Garth could not stay away from his music for long. By August 1992, he had released his first Christmas album, *Beyond the Season.* Its sales exceeded $3 million, and part of the

In addition to producing and performing in his own television specials, Garth is much sought after for guest appearances. Here, sporting a new cowboy hat, host Oprah Winfrey flashes a smile as Garth plays for her during a taping of her show in Amarillo, Texas.

proceeds benefited a charity called Feed the Children. "This is the most fun I have ever had making an album. Christmas albums are usually cut in the summer months, so our engineer, Mark Miller, strung Christmas light[s] all over the studio—it was great. I'd make this album every day of my life if I could because you're singing about what counts."

A month later, Garth again overwhelmed his fans with his fifth album, *The Chase.* Because the album was produced during 1991 and 1992, when his life was beginning to change, the songs bare much of Garth's soul. In a retrospective moment, speaking about this album, Garth confided:

> I opened myself completely on that album. It's the closest anybody has ever got to getting inside my head. So much was going on. We were expecting our first baby, trying to get our house remodeled, and I was out on the road all the time. The album was recorded during a time that I felt like maybe I couldn't have everything—a career and a family—and do it right. That was the time I thought about giving up the music if it was going to take me away from home too much, and the emotion showed. It was an important album for me to do, and I absolutely adore it.

Included in the album was "We Shall Be Free," which Garth and Stephanie Davis wrote after Garth witnessed the 1992 riots in Los Angeles. The song's theme proclaims that only when people see past sexual and racial prejudices will the nation truly be free. Three other hit singles from *The Chase* describe dramatically different romantic relationships, all of which tell of love, with its endurance, sometimes confusion, and sometimes heart-break. Country music has often been stigmatized as having the same "cry in your beer" lyrics over lost love. But Garth can take a shopworn story and bring it to life with his heartfelt emotion and unique lyrics, creating a song each listener can relate to and sympathize with.

Just before Garth kicked off his 1993–94 World Tour, he had released *In Pieces*, his sixth album. Garth explained the title: "We titled this album *In Pieces* because that's pretty much how it came together. We had more time with this album, and we had fun with it." Included in the album were several top-10 and number-one hits such as "Ain't Going Down (Til the Sun Comes Up)," "American Honky Tonk Bar Association," and "One Night a Day."

Further success followed in 1993 when it was announced that concerts to be held at the Dallas Cowboys' home, Texas Stadium, would be televised on another NBC special. Eager fans made these concerts the largest and fastest-selling by a country act in the United States. More than 65,000 tickets were sold in 92 minutes for Garth's first show. He continued to pull in a slew of awards for singing and performing and for his albums and singles. Among them was his third Entertainer of the Year award from the Academy of Country Music.

As if releasing six albums in five years was not enough, in 1994 Garth produced two more much-anticipated albums—collections of his greatest hits. The proceeds from the album

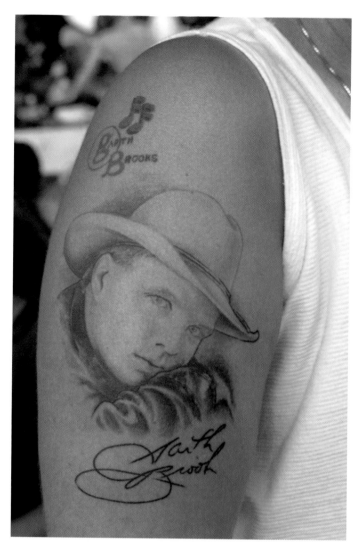

Garth fans go to great lengths to express their admiration. This fan honors his idol with a huge tattoo on his arm that even boasts Garth's signature.

The Garth Brooks Collection, which was sold only at McDonald's restaurants, benefited the Ronald McDonald Children's Charities. His second album, *The Hits*, was released for a limited time only. It sold more than nine million copies, becoming the best-selling "greatest hits" package in country music history.

Fans enjoyed still more of Garth that year

when he aired his second NBC special, *This Is Garth Brooks, Too.* Viewers again were overwhelmed by the enthusiasm and passion that Garth brings to his music and performances. This time, special effects included smoke, fire, and rain.

When Garth's second daughter, August Anna Brooks, was born that year, he again wanted to slow down to be with his growing family. Fans wondered if he would now decide it was time to retire.

7

THIS IS
GARTH BROOKS

S ome might say that Garth Brooks is addicted to his
audience. He cannot seem to get enough of them.
Barely finishing one concert, he is already planning his
next one. One album is released, and Garth is hard at
work on the follow-up. He often talks about slowing down,
but he rarely stops for long.

Having taken a year off from producing an album only
encouraged Garth's fans to anticipate the next one even
more. *Fresh Horses*, which was released in November
1995, reminded Garth of his first album because he was
starting up again. For Garth, taking time off meant he had
to start from the beginning and get his creative energies
flowing. The result was an album with six top-10 hits,
including "She's Every Woman," "The Fever," "Beaches of
Cheyenne," and one of Garth's most sentimental songs
ever, "The Change." He wrote "The Change" in response to
the Oklahoma City bombing and also turned it into a
video. Garth spoke openly about this song, saying that
it is "probably the most powerful song I have ever dealt
with and it speaks on a subject that is very close to me."

*Garth enjoys a rare quiet moment cuddling a pet opossum.
Throughout his career, he has used his music to try to show
who the person Garth Brooks really is—a man who cares pas-
sionately about his family, friends, and the people he loves to
entertain.*

Seated among tons of equipment, Garth gets ready to embark on his international tour that took him to 99 cities and thrilled fans world-wide with an unprece-dented 347 concerts.

It's hard to imagine after all of the awards he has won, albums he has sold, and attention that he has received, that Garth Brooks could be any more successful than he is. Apparently he can, for his career continues to climb. In 1995, Garth received a number of first-time honors. He was awarded the ACM's Jim Reeves Memorial award, an honor only given to an artist who is recognized as uniquely pro-moting and enhancing the image of country music internationally, and an award that had not been granted in 13 years. He also had his star placed on the Hollywood Walk of Fame and garnered numerous other national and international awards. In addition, his album sales exceeded the 60-million mark, making him the second-largest album-sales artist in the United States. Only The Beatles can claim higher sales.

Instead of releasing an album in 1996, Garth embarked on a world tour. Beginning in March, he visited 99 cities, where he performed a total of 347 concerts. The tour was his most extensive to date and was a tremendous undertaking in terms of the equipment and people needed to transport all the props and set everything up at each new location. Ten 18-wheelers carried the equipment and per-sonnel. In addition, Garth was joined for most of it by another very successful singer and friend, country music diva Trisha Yearwood. Audiences were delighted when they sang a few inspired duets together.

Garth has made two more albums since *Fresh Horses*. In 1997 he released *Sevens*, with six songs written by him, including the hits "Long Neck Bottle," "She's Gonna Make It," and "To Make You Feel My Love" (from the *Hope Floats* movie soundtrack). *Sevens* had the distinction of being the fastest-selling solo album ever. That same year, HBO aired a Garth Brooks concert live from New York City's Central Park. The show was the highest-rated and most-watched special on cable television in 1997.

A second album followed in 1998. Titled *Garth Brooks: Double Live*, it is a compilation of many of the concerts he has performed over the years. Thrilled fans could hear 25 songs with all the sound effects that make a Garth Brooks concert so appealing. Initially, the album boasted six different covers, each marking a special event or tour. "I can't tell you where we recorded it, because we recorded it in several different cities and sometimes they're pieced together," Garth says. "The live album is full of recordings that date all the way back to the Reunion Arena, but 90 percent of the live album was on this tour when we've been recording every night," he added. He might have added that the album is what Garth Brooks is all about—his live performances and his interaction with the fans.

Has Garth Brooks decided to take a well-deserved vacation? Is he getting ready for the millennium? Sort of. His main objective, he says, is "to be the best dad in the world," especially since he and Sandy had welcomed another daughter, Allie Colleen, while he was on tour in 1996. He is also taking some time to indulge in another of his passions—baseball. Accepting an invitation from the San Diego Padres, he joined them at their spring-training camp. Although Garth did not think he would make the team, he still wanted to "swing the bat for the sake of getting to hear the wood go through the wind."

Garth is having the time of his life playing baseball while at the same time helping others. Rather than paying him a salary, the Padres are donating $200,000 to the Touch 'Em All Foundation, a group of baseball players, entertainers, and corporations that raise money for children's charities.

Until he returns to the spotlight in the year 2000, Garth is involved in several projects. He is co-producing a feature film called *The Lamb.* With R&B star Kenny "Babyface" Edmonds, this thriller concerns a female fan's relationship with her music-star idol. Garth is also working on two more albums, one of which is *Colors of Christmas,* a holiday album that will also be a CBS-TV special. The other album is a long-promised set of duets with Trisha

Although Garth has taken time off to relax and be with his family, he is never really out of the spotlight. In early 1999, he appeared at the American Music Awards to enjoy a duet with country singer Trisha Yearwood.

Yearwood. And Garth is already itching to get back to writing songs for his next solo album.

Garth Brooks can best be described in one word—passionate. He is passionate about his music, his family, his desire to help others, and his fans. His own words best describe his love for his music: "If God came down here with the box that had the reason for living in it, I'd like to find just two words. The Music. That would be neat."

Garth's fans are well aware of how he feels about them from his live concerts, when he dashes around the stage and his eyes bulge with intensity. As one fan expressed it on a website: "Perhaps no entertainer has even connected as completely with his audience as has Garth Brooks. He loves them and they love him; together they form a circle of power and energy the likes of which you've never seen." He connects with his fans because he was once one of them. He remembered sitting in the cheap seats at a concert and wanting the singer to notice him and make him feel like part of the show. That memory follows him each time he steps out onto the stage to perform for thousands of screaming fans.

Garth's personal magic with an audience also includes focusing attention not only on fans in the front seats but also on those sitting in the "nose-bleed" sections as well. Before shows, Garth walks through the arenas and puts himself in his fans' seats to see the performance from their view. He also reserves a number of front-row seats at each of his shows and randomly picks a few fans from the highest sections to come on down and sit right up front.

Always overwhelmed by his fans' excitement and their support, Garth continually finds ways to thank them. Expressing his appreciation to his Irish fans who turned out in record numbers on his world tours, he wrote the song "Ireland" and included it on his *Fresh Horses* album. "I really want it to be like a postcard that thanks them," he said at the time. Fans could certainly tell how much he valued them when he showed up at Nashville's Fan Fair in 1996 and signed autographs for more than 23 hours.

In each album, Garth acknowledges everyone who has had a major impact on his life, including his band, crew, friends, others he works with, and especially his family. He takes every opportunity to pull Sandy onstage with him when he accepts an award. His daughters accompany him on tour whenever possible. And of course his own words reflect his passion for his loved ones. He wrote on the credits of his album *Fresh Horses*: "Sandy, will you marry me? Taylor and August, you're my reason why." Immediately after Taylor was born, Garth told *USA Today*: "I busted my butt to reach these goals, and then something like this happens and you feel very satisfied. The things I thought were the . . . important things aren't. Being a dad seems like a pretty full-time job." Bursting with pride, in his *Double Live* album, Garth poured out the depth of his feelings for his family: "My three daughters are the greatest thing I have ever been a part of," and later he adds, "All my love and thanks to: My wife, Sandy, your job is the toughest of all. Taylor, August, and Allie, your energy, innocence, and love are the things that give me strength."

Garth is just as passionate about his parents. Of his father he says, "If I could be like any man in the world, it would be him." He expressed his love for his mother in the best way a singer can by dedicating to her "It's Your Song" on his *Double Live* album. When he performs the song in concert, he can barely finish because he becomes so choked up. "A lady had written it for her mom, and her mom was a singer, and when it came my way, all I could see was my mom when I heard it," he explained. "She heard it the day before her surgery. . . . and it fits her to a T." Garth is referring to his mother's bout with cancer, one of the most difficult times he had to get through.

Still, there is another to whom Garth gives the most praise, which is reflected in such songs as "Unanswered Prayers" and "The River." He always saves his last thanks for God for His numerous blessings. Each credit in Garth's album end with the words "mostly, thanks to God, for it is through Him that all things are possible." A special note in his *Double Live* album reflects on the past decade: "to God and 'the people.' You are the reason for all things I treasure, I could never make You as happy as You have made me."

Garth is widely recognized for his charity to others and his desire to make the world a better place. In addition to performing benefit concerts and donating proceeds from albums to charities, he and Sandy dedicate much of their time to help at auctions, telethons, and other charity fundraisers. One story that illustrates Garth's compassion for others is told by the president of the Magic of Music

fund: "After driving into New Orleans from New York, Garth learned that an 11-year-old patient from the Monroe, Louisiana, area was unable to come to New Orleans to meet him. He got back on the bus and drove another five hours to go to her hospital room to personally meet her. This was not a request. This was something he decided was the right thing for him to do."

On May 5, 1999, Garth had the ultimate honor bestowed upon him. The Academy of

Being a star and celebrity has never diminished Garth's delight in his fans. His enthusiasm for the people who admire him is as great as theirs for him. Here he accommodates a crowd by stretching across his car to shake their hands.

Country Music selected him as the "Artist of the Decade" for having been the most outstanding and successful act during the 1990s, and having best exemplified, through appearances and recordings, the image of country music during the decade.

Despite his incredible success, Garth Brooks still worries that his popularity could just disappear at any time. He remains humble by being aware of this and through his belief that it was not necessarily his talents that put him at the top but simply being in the right place at the right time. "All of a sudden, there was pop in country music and we happened to be there when the wave hit," he says of his success with his band. "We weren't the cause of it, we just happened to be a victim of good timing. I don't know what happened, I'm just glad it happened to us."

Even if his popularity should fade one day, Garth says he would not change his life for anything. He is scared to death of losing his edge, but that has not stopped him and will not stop him from pursuing his passions. His message is clear: Don't wait for tomorrow to pursue your dreams, because "If Tomorrow Never Comes," you will have neglected the experience that is "The Dance."

CHRONOLOGY

1962   Troyal Garth Brooks is born on February 7 in Tulsa, Oklahoma.

1966   The Brooks family moves to Yukon, Oklahoma.

1980   Graduates from Yukon High School; enrolls at Oklahoma State University in Stillwater.

1982   Wins $50 first prize in university talent show playing guitar and singing; meets Sandy Mahl.

1984   Graduates from Oklahoma State University; records his first demo tape.

1985   Makes first trip to Nashville, Tennessee, but returns to Stillwater without success.

1986   Marries Sandy Mahl; manages a retail store; forms the band Santa Fe.

1987   Returns to Nashville with Sandy and his band; the band splits up; struggles to find a record deal.

1988   Signs with Major Bob Music, a music-publishing company; signs a contract with Capitol Records.

1989   Releases first single, which makes *Billboard*'s top-10 list; releases first album, *Garth Brooks*; tours to promote album; forms his new band, Stillwater; wins his first number-one single spot for "If Tomorrow Never Comes."

1990   Makes his first singing appearance at Fan Fair and receives his first gold album; releases his second album, *No Fences*; is inducted into the Grand Ole Opry as its 65th member.

1991   Is honored by the establishment of "Garth Brooks Day" in Yukon; releases third album, *Ropin' the Wind*.

1992   *This is Garth Brooks* NBC special airs; wins his first Grammy award for Best Vocal Performance by a Male Country Artist; appears on *Saturday Night Live*; begins his first national concert tour; releases albums *Beyond the Season* and *The Chase*; first child is born.

1993   Releases album *In Pieces*.

1994   Airs second NBC special, *This Is Garth Brooks, Too*; releases *The Garth Brooks Collection* and *The Hits*; second daughter is born.

1995	Releases album *Fresh Horses*; exceeds 60 million in album sales, becoming the second highest-selling artist in the United States.
1996	Tours internationally, performing 347 concerts in 99 cities; third daughter is born.
1997	Release album *Sevens*; airs *Garth—Live From Central Park* on HBO.
1998	Appears on *Saturday Night Live*; releases *Garth Brooks: Double Live*, his first album of live concerts.
1999	Takes a year off; joins the San Diego Padres' spring-training camp.

DISCOGRAPHY

1989	*Garth Brooks*
1990	*No Fences*
1991	*Ropin' The Wind*
1992	*Beyond The Season* *The Chase*
1993	*In Pieces*
1994	*The Garth Brooks Collection* *The Hits*
1995	*Fresh Horses*
1997	*Sevens*
1998	*Garth Brooks: Double Live*

AWARDS

1990	Video of the Year and Horizon award from Country Music Association (CMA); International Single of the Year from *Country Music People* (London) magazine; International Song of the Year from Nashville Songwriters Association.

1991	Video of the Year, Song of the Year, Single Record of the Year, Album of the Year, Male Vocalist of the Year, and Entertainer of the Year from ACM; Best Country Song of the Year from AMA; *Billboard* Music awards for Top Pop Album Artist, Top Country Artist, Top Country Album Artist, and Top Country Singles Artist; Album of the Year, Video of the Year, Single of the Year, and Entertainer of the Year awards from CMA; Juno award (Canada) for Foreign Entertainer of the Year; *Music City News/* Nashville Network Viewer's Choice award for Video of the Year; NARM Best Seller awards for Record of the Year, Recording by a Male Artist, Country Music Recording by a Male Artist, and Music Video; Performer of the Year, Best Single, and Best Album from *Radio & Records* Readers Poll.
1992	Special Achievement, Male Vocalist of the Year, Entertainer of the Year, and Best Country Album of the Year awards from ACM; Best Country Song of the Year from AMA; No. 1 Pop Album Artist, No. 1 *Billboard* 200 Album, No. 1 *Billboard* 200 Album Artist, No. 1 Country Artist, No. 1 Hot Country Singles Artist, No. 1 Country Album, and No. 1 Country Album Artist awards from *Billboard*; Album of the Year and Entertainer of the Year from CMA; Male Vocalist and Album of the Year from Country Music People's International; Male Vocalist of the Year from The Dutch Country Music awards; Top Male Singer from *Entertainment Weekly*'s Reader's Poll; Grammy award for Best Male Country Vocal Performance; Entertainer of the Year from *Music City News*/TNN Viewer's Choice awards; Artist of the Year from Music Row Industry Summit awards; Best Male Country Performer and Best Male Musical Performer from People's Choice awards; Country Artist of the Year from *Performance* magazine; Major Tour of the Year award from *Pollstar* magazine; Performer of the Year, Male Vocalist of the Year, Single of the Year, and Album of the Year from *Radio & Records* Readers Poll; *Rolling Stone* magazine Reader's Choice award for Country Artist of the Year; World Music award for Best Selling Country Artist.
1993	Entertainer of the Year from ACM; Best Country Music Male Performer from AMA; *Billboard* awards for No. 1 Pop Artist, No. 1 *Billboard* 200 Album Artist, No. 1 Country Artist, No. 1 Country

Album Artist, and No. 1 Hot Country Singles Artist; Best Male Country Vocalist from *Playboy* Annual Reader Poll; People's Choice awards for Male Musical Performer and Male Country Music Performer; Country Artist of the Year from *Performance* magazine Reader's Poll; Major Tour of the Year from *Pollstar* magazine; Performer of the Year from *Radio & Records* Readers Poll; Country Artist of the Year from *Rolling Stone* Readers' Poll; Best Male Singer and Outstanding Recording award from *US* magazine Poll; World Music award for Best Selling Country Artist.

1994   Video of the Year and Entertainer of the Year from ACM; Best Country Male Vocalist from AMA; *Billboard* awards for No. 1 Country Album Artist, No. 1 Country Male Artist; Dutch Country Music award for Best Male Vocalist; People's Choice award for Best Male Musical Performer; Best Male Musical Performer from *Radio & Records* Readers Poll; World Music award for Best Selling Artist.

1995   Best Country Male Vocalist from AMA; People's Choice award for Best Male Musical Performer; Video of the Year and Jim Reeves Memorial award from ACM; Best Male Singer from *US* magazine; Great Britain's Country Music awards for International Male Vocalist, Best Touring Act, and International Album; World Music award for Best Selling Country Artist.

1996   Album of the Year, Favorite Male Country Artist, and Favorite Artist of the Year from AMA; People's Choice award for Favorite Country Male Vocalist; Canadian Country Music award for Top Selling Album; World Music award for World's Best Selling Country Male Artist.

1997   Favorite Male Country Artist from AMA; Entertainer of the Year from CMA; *Billboard* music award for Special Achievement in Music; People's Choice award for Favorite Country Male Vocalist.

1998   Grammy awards for Best Country Collaboration With Vocals and Best Vocal Collaboration; Favorite Male Artist from *People* magazine; Special Achievement and Entertainer of the Year awards from CMA.

1999   Entertainer of the Year and Artist of the Decade awards from CMA.

Further Reading

"Encore! Garth's Tour is Over—But He's Not Disappearing." *Country Weekly*, November 17, 1998.

Howey, Paul. *Garth Brooks: Chart-Bustin' Country.* Minneapolis: Lerner Publications Company, 1998.

Morris, Edward. *Garth Brooks: Platinum Cowboy.* New York: St. Martin's Press, 1993.

Wallner, Rosemary. *Garth Brooks: Country Music Star.* Minneapolis: Abdo Consulting Group, Inc., 1993.

Websites

www.americanmusicawards.com [American Music Association's homepage]

www.cma.com [Country Music Association's homepage]

www.planetgarth.com. [Garth Brooks unofficial website]

About the Author

STACEY L. STAUFFER has a degree in English and a concentration in creative writing and communications from Ursinus College in Collegeville, Pennsylvania. Several of her poems and short stories have been published in literary magazines, and her articles have been printed in local publications, including the *Chester County Press* and a multicultural newspaper, *La Voz*. She has written several books for Chelsea House. She has worked as a journalist, freelance writer, and editor, and currently works in marketing.

INDEX

Academy of Country Music awards, 8-11, 33-34, 45, 50-51, 58

"Ain't Going Down (Til the Sun Comes Up)", 45

"American Honky Tonk Bar Association," 45

"Beaches of Cheyenne," 49

Best Video of the Year award, 8

Beyond the Season, 44

Black, Clint, 7, 33

Brooks, Allie Colleen (daughter), 52, 55

Brooks, Anna (daughter), 47, 55

Brooks, Betsy (sister), 14, 33

Brooks, Colleen Carroll (mother), 13, 14, 15-17, 19, 56

Brooks, Garth
  birth of, 13
  childhood of, 13-16
  children of, 42, 47, 52, 55
  education of, 14-15, 16-17, 19-23
  family of, 13-14, 15-17, 55-56
  and fans, 54-55
  media coverage of, 42-43
  as movie producer, 53
  and retirement, 42-43, 47
  and sports, 14-15, 16, 17, 19, 52
  and start of career, 16, 19-23
  style of, 28, 29, 52, 54
  and TV specials, 41-42, 45, 47, 51
  vocal heroes of, 9-10, 22-23
  and wife (Sandy Mahl), 20-22, 23, 25, 26, 30, 33, 38, 42, 55

Brooks, Kelly (brother), 13, 17, 19, 33

Brooks, Taylor Mayne Pearl (daughter), 42, 55

Brooks, Troyal Raymond (father), 13, 14, 15-17, 56

Capitol Records, 27-30

"Change, The," 49

"Change, The" (video), 49

Chase, The, 44-45

Color of Christmas, 53

Country Music Association awards, 7-11, 36, 39

"Dance, The," 34, 58

"Dance, The" (video), 34, 35-36

Davis, Stephanie, 44

Double Live, 55, 56

Doyle, Bob, 26, 27-28

Dunn, Holly, 34

Farm Aid, 34

Feed the Children, 44

"Fever, The," 49

Fogelberg, Dan, 20, 21

Foglesong, Jim, 27-28

Fresh Horses, 49, 55

"Friends in Low Places," 7, 37

Frost, Lane, 36

Garth Brooks, 29, 36-37, 38

Garth Brooks: Double Live, 51-52

Garth Brooks Collection, The, 46

Haggard, Merle, 22

Harris, Jim, 20, 23

Hits, The, 46-47

Hollywood Walk of Fame, 51

Horizon Award, 8

"If Tomorrow Never Comes," 28, 29-30, 58

In Pieces, 45

"Ireland," 55

"It's Your Song," 56

Jones, George, 9-10, 22

Lamb, The (movie), 53

LeDoux, Chris, 34

"Long Neck Bottle," 51

McEntire, Reba, 7, 34

Magic of Music fund, 56-57

Mahl, Sandy (wife), 20-22, 23, 25, 26, 30, 33, 38, 42, 55

"Much Too Young," 29

No Fences, 37-38, 39

Oklahoma State University, 17, 19-23

Reynolds, Allen, 28-29

"River, The," 56

Ronald McDonald Children's Charities, 46

Ropin' the Wind, 38-39

San Diego Padres, 52

Santa Fe (band), 26

Sevens, 51

"She's Every Woman," 49

"She's Gonna Make It," 51

Shults, Lynn, 28

Skinner Brothers (band), 26

Stillwater (band), 29

Strait, George, 9-10, 22-23

Thunder Rolls, 7

"Thunder Rolls, The," 37

"Thunder Rolls, The" (video), 37-38

"To Make You Feel My Love," 51

Touch 'Em All Foundation, 52

"Two of a Kind," 37

"Unanswered Prayers," 37, 56

"Unwound," 23

"We Shall Be Free," 44-45

"Workin' on a Full House," 37

World Tours, 45, 51

Yearwood, Trisha, 51, 53-54